This book belongs to:

For two dear friends in our publishing family: Liz Johnson and LeeEric Fesko. Thanks for all you do to help so many.

Itsy Bitsy Christmas

© 2013 by Max Lucado.

Karen Hill, Executive Editor for Max Lucado.

Illustrated by Bruno Merz.

Published in Nashville, Tennessee, by Tommy Nelson. Tommy Nelson is a registered trademark of Thomas Nelson, Inc.

Tommy Nelson, Inc., titles may be purchased in bulk for educational, business, fund-raising, or sales promotional use. For information, please e-mail SpecialMarkets@ThomasNelson.com.

ISBN-13 978-1-4003-2262-6 (hardcover)
ISBN-13 978-1-4003-2404-0 (international edition)

Library of Congress Cataloging-in-Publication Data

Lucado, Max.
  Itsy Bitsy Christmas / by Max Lucado ; illustrated by Bruno Merz.
    pages cm
  Summary: When a donkey tells Itsy and Bitsy, brother and sister mice, that a king is coming to Bethlehem they set out
    to find him, even though their friends tell them no king would ever come to so small and common a place.
    ISBN 978-1-4003-2262-6 (jacketed hardcover) 1. Jesus Christ—Nativity—Juvenile fiction. [1. Jesus Christ—Nativity—
    Fiction. 2. Brothers and sisters—Fiction. 3. Mice—Fiction. 4. Animals—Fiction.] I. Merz, Bruno, 1976– illustrator. II.
    Title.
PZ7.L9684Its 2013
[E]—dc23
                                                                                                      2013001047

Printed in China

13 14 15 16 17 TIMS 6 5 4 3 2 1

Itsy Bitsy
CHRISTMAS

BY MAX LUCADO

Illustrated by Bruno Merz

Tommy
NELSON

A Division of Thomas Nelson Publishers

NASHVILLE   DALLAS   MEXICO CITY   RIO DE JANEIRO

Bitsy, watch out!" Itsy grabbed his little sister's tail and pulled her back just in time. The big wagon rolled past and splashed them with mud. "Be careful, Bitsy. You don't want to get run over."

Bitsy jumped back and gulped. Her big eyes grew even wider.

"I've never seen Bethlehem so busy!" she exclaimed. "People everywhere. Wagons rolling. Cows mooing. Donkeys pulling. And camels . . . do you know that camels spit?" Bitsy stepped away from the camel nearest her. "What is going on, Itsy?"

"Follow me, and I'll show you," the older mouse replied.

Itsy took his sister's hand, and they scampered to the top of the city wall. "It is time to count all the people. Everyone has to go to their hometown and sign the big book."

Bitsy looked around. "This is a big day for Bethlehem."

"Big day, indeed," said a deep voice behind them. Itsy and Bitsy turned. A donkey was talking to them. The mice were on the wall, so they could see him face-to-face.

"Whoa, you're big!" said Itsy. "I've never seen inside the nose of a donkey," he added, peering inside the nostril.

"Eeweey," Bitsy offered.

"Who are you?" she asked the donkey.

"I'm Daniel from a faraway town."

"Are you here to be counted?"

"No," he said very slowly. "I am here because of the King."

"What?"

"Haven't you heard? The King is coming to Bethlehem."

"But Bethlehem is an itsy bitsy town," Bitsy explained. "Why would a King come here?"

"This King is special. He comes for everyone, big and small."

"Like us?" Itsy asked.

"Like you."

Bitsy turned, her whiskers bouncing.
"Itsy, we need to tell our friends!"
"Yes, yes!" Itsy agreed. "They will want
to see the King too!"

The mice dashed between feet,
hooves, and rolling wagon wheels and
ran toward their stable.

They scurried under the gate, up the
stable post, and onto their favorite rafter.

From their spot high above the floor, they could see all
their friends. Ruthie the mama horse was the biggest.
Rowdy the rooster was perched on the rail. Six sheep
were crowded in the corner. Charlie the cow grazed on
some hay. Grumpy the goat sulked in another corner.
He never smiled. He was always mad at someone.

Itsy cupped his hands over his mouth and squeaked, "Okay, everyone, gather in. We need to talk." No one moved.

Bitsy tried, "We have big news!"

No response.

Bitsy turned to Rowdy the rooster. "Can you help us?"

"Sure," replied Rowdy. "I love any excuse to make some noise." He leaned his head back—

"Cock-a-doodle-doooooo!!!"

The animals lifted their heads. "Hey," groaned
Grumpy the goat. "Knock it off. I'm trying to nap."
"Itsy and I have big news!"
"You're moving?" Grumpy muttered.
"Grumpy, be nice," said Ruthie the mama horse.
"Itsy and Bitsy, tell us your big news."

"A King is coming to Bethlehem. To us!"
No one spoke for a long time. Then Rowdy crowed,
"A King to Bethlehem? That will never happen."
The others snorted, baahed, neighed, and mooed
in agreement.

"Kings come to important places," offered the sheep.

"And to important people," agreed Grumpy. "Not to places like Bethlehem or to mice like you."

"Itsy and Bitsy," Ruthie the mama horse spoke up, "I'm afraid this place is too common for a King. No King would care about us."

Itsy looked at Bitsy. "Well . . . Bitsy and I are going to find the King."

"Good luck with that," chuckled Grumpy.

"To see the King! To see the King!" Bitsy zipped down the post and out into the street, but then she stopped. "Itsy, where will we find Him?"

Itsy paused for a moment, placing his finger on his chin. "Well, let's go where the important people go. To the city gate!"

Off they went. The leaders of the town sat at the city gate, making decisions. Bitsy spotted a wise owl sitting on top of the gate. "Mr. Owl," she shouted, "we hear that a King is coming to Bethlehem. Have you seen Him?"

"A King in tiny little Bethlehem? You won't find a King here."

So the King hadn't come to the wise ones at the city gate.

"I know," Itsy offered. "Let's go where the camels live. Kings ride on camels, right?" So the two mice scampered over to the camel corral.

"Mr. Camel," shouted Itsy, "we are looking for a King. Have you seen Him?"

"Silly mouse. I've carried some very rich and important men in my day, but I assure you, they didn't come here. Kings don't come to common places like Bethlehem."

"But we talked to a donkey and . . ."

"Humph. Never trust a donkey," snickered the camel.

Itsy sighed. "Where else can we look?"

"Well, let's look everywhere," said Bitsy.

The mice ran to the main street where the busy people rushed around. Lots of busy people, but no King.

They ran to the hotel where the sleepy people spent time resting. Lots of sleepy people, but no King.

They ran to the city market where the business people worked all day. Lots of working people, but no King.

Finally, Itsy and Bitsy began to get tired. It was getting dark. "Let's go home, Bitsy," Itsy sighed. "Everyone is right. No King is coming for us. We aren't important enough."

Bitsy started to object but didn't. A tear formed on her cheek as they headed toward home. "I always wanted to see a King. Now I guess I never will."

But when the mice neared the stable, they saw Daniel the donkey, the same one who had told them about the King. Itsy and Bitsy ran up onto the stable fence. "We have looked all over town for the King. We couldn't find Him."

"Well," said the donkey in his low, slow voice, "you just did."

Daniel motioned with his head to the center of the stable where all the animals stood in a circle. The two mice scampered up a fence post and looked.

A little Baby was asleep in the manger.

"Who is He?" asked Itsy.

"He is the King," replied Ruthie. "Just like you said, a King came to Bethlehem."

"His name is Jesus," explained Daniel the donkey. "God sent Him to love us, help us, and save us."

"He came for me, even though I laughed at you?" asked Rowdy the rooster.

"And for us? Even though we doubted you?" asked the sheep.

"And me? I can get cranky," admitted Grumpy.

Daniel smiled and nodded his big head. "God sent Jesus for us all."

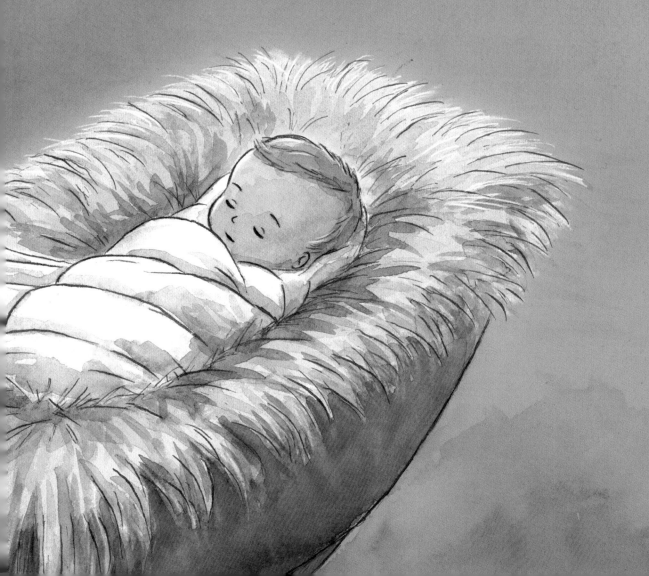

"Who would have thought?" observed Itsy.
"A King for everyone."

A tiny tear of joy rolled all the way down
Bitsy's nose. "He came," Bitsy said with a smile.

"Even for a little one like me!"